How to Sample in Surveys

2nd edition

THE SURVEY KIT, Second Edition

Purposes: The purposes of this 10-volume Kit are to enable readers to prepare and conduct surveys and to help readers become better users of survey results. Surveys are conducted to collect information; surveyors ask questions of people on the telephone, face-to-face, and by mail. The questions can be about attitudes, beliefs, and behavior as well as socioeconomic and health status. To do a good survey, one must know how to plan and budget for all survey tasks, how to ask questions, how to design the survey (research) project, how to sample respondents, how to collect reliable and valid information, and how to analyze and report the results.

Users: The Kit is for students in undergraduate and graduate classes in the social and health sciences and for individuals in the public and private sectors who are responsible for conducting and using surveys. Its primary goal is to enable users to prepare surveys and collect data that are accurate and useful for primarily practical purposes. Sometimes, these practical purposes overlap with the objectives of scientific research, and so survey researchers will also find the Kit useful.

Format of the Kit: All books in the series contain instructional objectives, exercises and answers, examples of surveys in use and illustrations of survey questions, guidelines for action, checklists of dos and don'ts, and annotated references.

Volumes in The Survey Kit:

1. **The Survey Handbook, 2nd**
   Arlene Fink
2. **How to Ask Survey Questions, 2nd**
   Arlene Fink
3. **How to Conduct Self-Administered and Mail Surveys, 2nd**
   Linda B. Bourque and Eve P. Fielder
4. **How to Conduct Telephone Surveys, 2nd**
   Linda B. Bourque and Eve P. Fielder
5. **How to Conduct In-Person Interviews for Surveys, 2nd**
   Sabine Mertens Oishi
6. **How to Design Survey Studies, 2nd**
   Arlene Fink
7. **How to Sample in Surveys, 2nd**
   Arlene Fink
8. **How to Assess and Interpret Survey Psychometrics, 2nd**
   Mark S. Litwin
9. **How to Manage, Analyze, and Interpret Survey Data, 2nd**
   Arlene Fink
10. **How to Report on Surveys, 2nd**
    Arlene Fink

Arlene Fink

How to Sample in Surveys

2nd edition

THE SURVEY KIT
TSK 2

SAGE Publications
International Educational and Professional Publisher
Thousand Oaks ▪ London ▪ New Delhi

For information:

Sage Publications, Inc.
2455 Teller Road
Thousand Oaks, California 91320
E-mail: order@sagepub.com

Sage Publications Ltd.
6 Bonhill Street
London EC2A 4PU
United Kingdom

Sage Publications India Pvt. Ltd.
M-32 Market
Greater Kailash I
New Delhi 110 048 India

Printed in the United States of America

Library of Congress Cataloging-in-Publication Data

The survey kit.—2nd ed.
    p. cm.
Includes bibliographical references.
ISBN 0-7619-2510-4 (set : pbk.)
1. Social surveys. 2. Health surveys. I. Fink, Arlene.
HN29 .S724 2002
300'.723—dc21   2002012405

This book is printed on acid-free paper.

02 03 04 05 10 9 8 7 6 5 4 3 2 1

Acquisitions Editor:	C. Deborah Laughton
Editorial Assistant:	Veronica Novak
Copy Editor:	Judy Selhorst
Production Editor:	Diane S. Foster
Typesetter:	Bramble Books
Proofreader:	Cheryl Rivard
Cover Designer:	Ravi Balasuriya
Production Designer:	Michelle Lee

Contents

How to Sample in Surveys:
Learning Objectives

The aim of this book is to guide you in selecting and using appropriate sampling methods. The specific objectives are as follows:

- Distinguish between target populations and samples

  - Identify research questions and survey objectives

  - Specify inclusion and exclusion criteria

- Choose the appropriate probability and nonprobability sampling methods

  - Simple random sampling

  - Stratified random sampling

  - Systematic sampling

  - Cluster sampling

  - Convenience sampling

  - Snowball sampling

  - Quota sampling

  - Focus groups

- Understand the logic in estimating standard errors
- Understand the logic in sample size determinations
- Understand the logic in determining sample size, so you have the power to detect a difference if one exists

- Understand the sources of error in sampling
- Calculate the response rate

1

Target Populations and Samples

A sample is a portion or subset of a larger group called a *population*. The population is the universe to be sampled, such as all Americans, all residents of California during the 1994 earthquake, or all people over 85 years of age. Survey researchers often study samples rather than whole populations.

A good sample is a miniature version of the population of which it is a part—just like it, only smaller. The best sample is **representative**, or a model, of the population. A sample is representative if important characteristics (e.g., age, gender, health status) of those within the sample are distributed similarly to the way they are distributed in the larger population. Suppose the population of interest consists of 1,000 people, 50% of whom are male and 45% of whom are over 65 years of age. A representative sample will have fewer people (say, 500), but it also consists of 50% males and 45% over the age of 65.

Survey samples are not meaningful in themselves. The importance of a sample lies in the accuracy with which it represents or mirrors the **target population**, which consists of the institutions, persons, problems, and systems to which or to whom the survey's findings are to be applied or *generalized*. Consider the two surveys described in Example 1.1. In Survey 1, 500 parents will be sampled, and their responses will be used to represent the views of the target population: all parents whose children are in the district's elementary schools. In Survey 2, 200 persons will represent the target population of all library users who check out books.

EXAMPLE 1.1
Two Surveys:
Target Populations and Samples

Survey 1

General Purpose: To examine the attitudes of parents regarding the introduction of new dietary and nutritional programs into elementary schools

Target Population: All parents of children in a school district's elementary schools

Sample: 500 of the district's 10,000 parents (100 chosen at random from each of the district's five elementary schools)

Survey 2

General Purpose: To compare the reading habits of different users of the local library

Target Population: All persons who check out books from the library

Sample: Over the course of an allotted 6-month period, the first 200 of all persons who check out books and complete the survey

Why should you sample? Why not include all parents and all people who check out books in these two studies, for example? Sampling allows for efficiency and precision in a survey study. Samples can be studied more quickly than entire target populations, and they are also less expensive to assemble. Sampling is efficient in that resources that might go into collecting data on an unnecessarily large number of individuals or groups can be spent on other activities, such as monitoring the quality of data collection.

Sampling helps to focus a survey on precisely the characteristics of interest. For example, if you want to compare older and younger parents of differing ethnicities, sampling strategies are available (in this case, stratified sampling) to give you just what you need. In many cases, it is more suitable for survey researchers to examine a sample of the population with precisely defined characteristics than to try to look at the entire population.

When selecting a sample, you should make sure that it is a faithful representation of the target population. No sample is perfect, however; almost every sample has some degree of bias or error. Use the following checklist to help ensure that your sample has characteristics and a degree of representation that you can describe accurately.

Checklist for Obtaining a Sample That Represents the Target

✓ State your survey objectives precisely.

The objectives are the reasons for doing the survey. Surveys are done to describe, compare, and predict knowledge, attitudes, and behavior. For example, a company might conduct a survey of its employees to gather data that will describe employees' educational backgrounds and preferences for work schedules and enable human resources personnel to compare employees on

---

these characteristics. School administrators might have surveyors conduct interviews with students and use the data to help predict the courses that are likely to have the most influence on students' future plans.

Researchers also use survey data to evaluate whether particular programs and policies have been effective. For example, a company's management may be interested in investigating whether employee morale has improved 3 years after the firm's reorganization, and school officials may want to know how students in a new ethics education program compare with those who have not been exposed to the program in terms of their goals and aspirations. If surveys involve self-administered questionnaires and/or interviews, they are being used for research purposes (*research* is used here in a very general way to include systematic inquiries or investigations).

Example 1.2 illustrates how the general purposes of the two surveys described in Example 1.1, of parents' attitudes toward nutrition programs and of the reading habits of library users, might be further refined into specific objectives and research questions.

EXAMPLE 1.2
General Purposes, Specific Objectives, and Research Questions

Survey 1

General Purpose: To examine the attitudes of parents regarding the introduction of new dietary and nutritional programs into elementary schools

Specific Objective: To describe and compare the attitudes of parents of differing ages, ethnicities, and knowledge of nutrition toward the introduction of three

Example 1.2 continued

new dietary and nutrition plans under considera-
tion by the schools

Specific Research Questions:

1. What are the attitudes of parents of differing
   ages toward the introduction of three new
   dietary and nutrition plans?

2. What are the attitudes of parents of differing
   ethnicities toward the introduction of three
   new dietary and nutrition plans?

3. Do parents who know more about nutrition
   differ from other parents in their attitudes?

Survey 2

General Purpose: To compare the reading habits of different users of the local library

Specific Objective: To compare reading habits among local
library users of differing ages, genders, and educational attainment

Specific Research Questions:

1. Do differences exist between older users and
   younger users in terms of reading habits?

2. Do differences exist between males and
   females in terms of reading habits?

3. Do differences exist among people of differing educational levels in terms of reading
   habits?

The specific research questions established are the guide to the specific questions or items that must be included in the survey. Given the research questions stated for Survey 1 in Example 1.2, the survey must include questions about the respondent's age and ethnicity and questions that test the respondent's knowledge of nutrition. Survey 2 must include questions about the respondent's age, gender, education, and reading habits.

EXERCISE

Add at least one possible research question to Surveys 1 and 2 in Example 1.2.

● ●
POSSIBLE ANSWERS

For Survey 1: Do parents of older children and younger children differ in their attitudes?

For Survey 2: Which are the most important factors in predicting reading habits: age, gender, and/or educational attainment?

✓ Establish clear and definite eligibility criteria.

Eligibility or inclusion criteria are the characteristics a person must have in order to be eligible for participation in the survey; exclusion criteria are those characteristics that rule out certain people. You apply your inclusion and exclusion criteria to the target population, and once you have removed from that population all those who fail to meet the inclusion criteria and all those who succeed in meeting the exclusion criteria, you are left with a study population consisting of people who are eligible to participate. Consider the illustrations in Example 1.3.

EXAMPLE 1.3
Inclusion and Exclusion Criteria:
Who Is Eligible?

Research Question: How effective is QUITNOW in helping smokers stop smoking?

Target Population: Smokers

Inclusion Criteria:
- Between the ages of 18 and 64 years
- Smoke one or more cigarettes daily
- Have an alveolar breath carbon monoxide determination of more than eight parts per million

Exclusion Criterion: Have any of the contraindications for the use of nicotine gum

Comment: The survey's results will apply only to persons who are eligible to participate. The findings may not apply to any smokers under 18 years of age or 65 or over. Although the target population is smokers, the inclusion and exclusion criteria define their own world, or study population, as "people ages 18 through 64 who smoke one or more cigarettes a day, have an alveolar breath carbon monoxide determination of more than eight parts per million, and do not have any of the contraindications for the use of nicotine gum."

Example 1.3 continued

Research Question: Are parents of elementary school children satisfied with the school district's new reading curriculum?

Target Population: Parents with children in elementary school in the district of interest

Inclusion Criteria:
- Have a child who has spent at least 6 months in one of the district's elementary schools as of April 15
- Speak English or Spanish

Exclusion Criterion: Inability or unwillingness to participate in a telephone or in-person interview in the 4 weeks beginning May 1

Comment: The target population is parents with children in elementary school. Parents who do not speak English or Spanish or who are unable to participate in an interview are not eligible to be part of the study population.

Both of the surveys in Example 1.3 set boundaries concerning who is eligible to be a respondent. In so doing, they also limit the generalizability of the survey findings. Why would surveyors deliberately limit the applicability of their findings?

A major reason for setting eligibility criteria is that to do otherwise is simply not practical. Including all smokers under the age of 18 and ages 65 and over in the survey of smokers would require additional resources for administering the survey and for analyzing and interpreting the data gathered from large numbers of people.

Also, the needs of very young and very old smokers may be different from those of the majority of adult smokers. For the survey of elementary school children's parents, including those who speak only languages other than English and Spanish, it would require translation of the survey, an often difficult and costly task. Setting inclusion and exclusion criteria is an efficient way of focusing the survey on just those people from whom you are equipped to get the most accurate information.

EXERCISE

Directions: Set inclusion and exclusion criteria for the survey of library users (Survey 2) described in Example 1.1.

● ●
POSSIBLE ANSWERS

Inclusion Criteria:
- Must use the library within a 6-month period beginning with today's date
- Must check out a book for 24 hours or more
- Must hold a permanent library card

Exclusion Criterion:
- Not a member of the local community (e.g., relies on interlibrary loans)

Choose a rigorous sampling method.

Sampling methods are usually divided into two types: probability sampling and nonprobability sampling. **Probability sampling** provides a statistical basis for saying that a sample is representative of the study or target population. In probability sampling, every member of the target population has a known, nonzero probability of being included in the sample. Probability sampling implies the use of random selection, which eliminates subjectivity in choosing a sample. It is a "fair" way of getting a sample.

Nonprobability sampling is sampling in which participants are chosen based on the researcher's judgment regarding the characteristics of the target population and the needs of the survey. In nonprobability sampling, some members of the eligible target population have a chance of being chosen and others do not. Owing to chance, the survey's findings may not be applicable to the target group at all.

Probability Sampling

SIMPLE RANDOM SAMPLING

The first step in sampling is to obtain a list of the eligible units that compose a population from which to sample. If the sample is to be representative of the population from which it is selected, this list, or **sampling frame**, must include all or nearly all members of the population. In simple **random sampling**, every subject or unit has an equal chance of being selected from the sampling frame. Members of the target population are selected one at a time and independently. Once they have been selected, they are not eligible for a second chance and are not returned to the pool. Because of this equality of opportunity, random samples are considered relatively unbiased. One typical way of selecting a simple random sample is to apply random numbers (from a table or a computer-generated list) to lists of prospective participants.

Suppose you want to select the names of 10 employees at random, using a table of random numbers, from a list containing the names of 20 employees. The 20 names are the target population, and the list of names is the sampling frame. You begin by assigning each name on the list a number from 01 to 20 (e.g., Adams = 01, Baker = 02, and so on, through Zinsser = 20). You then choose the first 10 digits between 01 and 20 from the table of random numbers (such tables are found in almost all statistics textbooks). Alternatively, you could use a computer to generate 10 numbers between 01 and 20 at random. Suppose the numbers chosen by the computer are 01, 03, 05, 06, 12, 14, 15, 17, 19, and 20. The employees whose names have been assigned the corresponding numbers are included in the sample. For example, Adams and Zinsser, with numbers 01 and 20, are included; Baker (02) is not.

The advantage of simple random sampling is that you can get an unbiased sample without much technical difficulty. Unfortunately, random sampling may not pick up all of the elements in a population that are of interest. Suppose that you are conducting a survey of patient satisfaction, and that you have evidence from a previous study that older and younger patients usually differ substantially in their levels of satisfaction. If you use a simple random sample in your new survey, you might not pick up a large enough proportion of younger patients to detect any differences that matter in your particular survey. To be sure that you get adequate proportions of people with certain characteristics, you need to use stratified random sampling.

STRATIFIED RANDOM SAMPLING

In **stratified random sampling,** the population is divided into subgroups, or strata, and a random sample is then selected from each subgroup. For example, suppose you want to find out about the effectiveness of a program to teach men about options for the treatment of prostate cancer. You plan to survey a sample of 1,800 of the 3,000 men who have participated in the program. You also intend to divide the men into groups according to their general health status (as indicated by scores on a 32-item test), age, and income (high = +, medium = 0, and low = –). Health status, age, and income are the strata. Example 1.4 displays the sampling blueprint for this survey.

EXAMPLE 1.4
Sampling Blueprint for a Program to Educate Men About Options for Prostate Cancer Treatment

Scores and Income	Age (Years)					
	< 55	56-65	66-70	71-75	> 75	Total
25-32 points						
High income	30	30	30	30	30	150
Average	30	30	30	30	30	150
Low	30	30	30	30	30	150
17-24 points						
High income	30	30	30	30	30	150
Average	30	30	30	30	30	150
Low	30	30	30	30	30	150
9-16 points						
High income	30	30	30	30	30	150
Average	30	30	30	30	30	150
Low	30	30	30	30	30	150
1-8 points						
High income	30	30	30	30	30	150
Average	30	30	30	30	30	150
Low	30	30	30	30	30	150
Total	360	360	360	360	360	1,800

When you use stratified random sampling, how do you decide what the subgroups or strata should be? Strata should be chosen based on available evidence that they are related to the outcome, such as the treatment options chosen by men with prostate cancer. In this case, studies have shown that general health status, age, and income influence men's choices of treatment. Justification for the selection of particular strata can come from the literature and/or from expert opinion.

Stratified random sampling is more complicated than simple random sampling. The strata must be identified and justified, and using many subgroups can lead to large, unwieldy, and expensive surveys.

SYSTEMATIC SAMPLING

Suppose you have a list of the names of 3,000 customers from which a sample of 500 is to be selected for a marketing survey. Dividing 3,000 by 500 yields 6. That means that 1 of every 6 persons on the list will be in the sample. To sample systematically from the list, you need a random start. To obtain this, you can toss a die. Suppose the toss comes up with the number 5. This means that you select the 5th name on the list first, then the 11th, the 17th, the 23rd, and so on, until you have selected 500 names.

You should not use **systematic sampling** if repetition is a natural component of the sampling frame. For example, if the frame is a list of names, systematic sampling can result in a sample that lacks names that appear infrequently (e.g., names beginning with X). If the data are arranged by months and the interval is 12, the same months will be selected for each year. Features of the sampling frame such as infrequently appearing names and ordered data (e.g., January is always Month 1, December always Month 12) prevent each sampling unit (names or months) from having a chance of selection equal to that of every other unit. If systematic sampling is used without the guarantee that all units have an equal chance of selection, the resultant sample will not be a probability sample. When the sampling frame has no inherently recurring order, or you can reorder the list or adjust the sampling intervals, systematic sampling resembles simple random sampling.

CLUSTER SAMPLING

A cluster is a naturally occurring unit, such as a school or university (which has many classrooms, students, and teachers), a hospital, a city, or a state. In **cluster sampling**, clusters are randomly selected, and all members of selected clusters are included in the sample. For example, suppose that California's counties are trying out a new program to improve emergency care for critically ill and injured children. If you want to use cluster sampling, you can consider each county as a cluster and select and assign counties at random to the new children's emergency care program or to the traditional one. The programs in the selected counties would then be the focus of the survey.

Cluster sampling is used in large surveys. It differs from stratified sampling in that you start with a naturally occurring constituency. You then select from among the clusters and either survey all members of the selection or randomly select from among them. With stratified sampling, you create the groups. The difference between the two is illustrated in the two hypothetical cases described in Example 1.5.

EXAMPLE 1.5
Stratified and Cluster Sampling Contrasted

Case 1: Stratified Sampling

The employees of Microsell were grouped according to their departments (sales, marketing, research, and advertising), and 10 employees were selected at random from each department.

Example 1.5 continued

Case 2: Cluster Sampling

Five of the Foremost Hotel chain's 10 hotels were chosen at random, and all employees in the chosen hotels were surveyed.

Multistage sampling is an extension of cluster sampling in which clusters are selected and a sample is drawn from the cluster members by simple random sampling. Clustering and sampling can be done at any stage. Example 1.6 illustrates the use of cluster sampling in a survey of Italian parents' attitudes toward AIDS.

EXAMPLE 1.6
Cluster Sampling and Attitudes
of Italian Parents Toward AIDS

Social scientists from 14 of Italy's 21 regions surveyed parents of 725 students from 30 schools chosen by a cluster sample technique from among the 292 classical, scientific, and technical high schools in Rome. The survey staff visited the schools and selected students by using a list of random numbers based on the school's size. The selected students were given letters addressed to their parents that explained the goals of the study and stated when they would be contacted.

Cluster sampling and multistage sampling are efficient ways of collecting survey information when it is either impossible or impractical to compile an exhaustive list of the units constituting the target population. For example, it is unlikely that you can readily obtain lists of all patients in city hospitals, all members of sporting clubs, or all travelers to Europe, but you can more easily get lists of hospitals, official sporting clubs, and travel agents.

A general guideline to follow in multistage sampling is to maximize the number of clusters. As you increase the number of clusters, you can decrease the size of the sample within each. For example, suppose you plan to survey patient satisfaction with county hospitals and need a sample of 500 patients. If you include two hospitals, you will need to obtain 250 patients in each, a logistically difficult task to accomplish compared with obtaining 50 patients in each of 10 hospitals. In practice, you will have to decide which is more difficult to obtain: cooperation by hospitals or by patients?

Nonprobability Sampling

Surveyors sometimes use **nonprobability sampling** because the units appear representative or because they can be assembled conveniently. Nonprobability sampling is probably appropriate in at least three situations, as illustrated in Example 1.7. The subsections below describe six commonly used nonprobability sampling methods.

EXAMPLE 1.7
Three Appropriate Situations for the Use of Nonprobability Samples

1. *Surveys of Hard-to-Identify Groups.* A survey of the goals and aspirations of members of teenage gangs is conducted. Known gang members are asked to suggest at least three other gang members to be interviewed.

Example 1.7 continued

> *Comment:* It is not practical to implement a probability sampling method in this population because of potential difficulties in obtaining cooperation and completing interviews with all eligible respondents.

2. *Surveys of Specific Groups.* A survey of patients in the state's 10 hospices asks all who are capable of responding and willing to respond about pain and pain management.

> *Comment:* Because of ethical reasons, the surveyor may be reluctant to approach all eligible patients.

3. *Surveys in Pilot Situations.* A questionnaire is mailed to all 35 nurses who participated in a workshop to learn about the use of a computer in treating nursing home patients with fever. The survey's sponsors will use the results to help them decide whether to sponsor a formal trial and evaluation of the workshop with other nurses.

> *Comment:* The purpose of the survey is to gather information that will be used in decision making concerning whether or not the workshop should be formally tried out and evaluated. Because the data are to be used as part of planning activities and not to disseminate or advocate the workshop, a nonprobability sampling method is appropriate.

CONVENIENCE SAMPLING

A **convenience sample** consists of a group of individuals that is ready and available, as illustrated in Example 1.8. The convenience sample in this survey of the use of mental health services consists of all who are willing to be interviewed. People who voluntarily answer the survey's questions may be different in important ways from those who do not, however. For example, they may be more verbal, and this may affect their interest in and use of mental health services. Because of the potential for bias in the sampling method, the findings from this survey can be applied (and with great caution) only to low-income persons whose age, education, income, and so forth are similar to those in the convenience sample.

EXAMPLE 1.8
A Convenience Sample

Where do low-income people generally obtain mental health services, and how do they pay for them? To answer this question, a survey was conducted over a 2-week period, with interviewers posted in front of five supermarkets and five churches in an urban, low-income neighborhood. During the 2 weeks, 308 people completed the 10-minute survey.

SNOWBALL SAMPLING

In **snowball sampling**, previously identified members of a group are asked to identify other members of the population. As newly identified members name others, the sample snowballs. This technique is used when a population listing is unavailable and cannot be compiled. For example, teenage gang members and illegal aliens might be asked to participate in snowball sampling because there are no membership lists available for these groups. Snowball sampling is not used only with outlaws or unpopular people, however; Example 1.9 illustrates another possible use of this technique.

EXAMPLE 1.9
Snowball Sampling

A mail survey's aim is to identify the competencies that should be the focus of programs training generalist physicians for the next 20 years. The surveyors obtain a list of 50 physicians and medical educators, and they ask each of the 50 to nominate 5 others who would be likely to complete the questionnaire.

QUOTA SAMPLING

In **quota sampling**, you divide the population being studied into subgroups, such as male and female, younger and older. You then estimate the proportion of people in that population who fall into each subgroup (e.g., younger and older males and younger and older females). You then draw your sample to reflect the proportions you have estimated, as illustrated in Example 1.10.

EXAMPLE 1.10
Quota Sampling

An interview was conducted with a sample of boys and girls between the ages of 10 and 15. Based on estimates taken from school records, the researchers calculated the

Example 1.10 continued

proportion of children in the entire school district population who fell into each subgroup and made this table:

	Age (Years)					
Gender	10	11	12	13	14	15
% Boys	22	16	16	23	10	13
% Girls	12	25	12	24	10	7

Based on this table, 22% of the boys and 12% of the girls in the sample
should be 10 years old, 16% of the boys and 25% of the girls should be 11
years old, and so on.

For quota sampling to be effective, the proportions must
be accurate. Sometimes, this accuracy is elusive. School surveys, for example, are sometimes affected by mobile and
changing student populations; also, age distributions (such
as those in the table in Example 1.10) can vary considerably
from school to school.

FOCUS GROUPS

Marketing researchers often use **focus groups** to find out
what particular component of the public needs and will con-
sume. A focus group usually consists of 6 to 10 people who
are brought together to take part in a moderated group discussion; participants are chosen to represent a particular
population, such as teens, potential customers, or members
of a particular profession. Health and social science
researchers often use focus groups or variations on them in
survey studies when consumers, clients, or patients are the
focus of their interest, as illustrated in Example 1.11.

Focus groups can result in relatively in-depth portraits of
the needs and expectations of specific populations. If the

EXAMPLE 1.11
Focus Groups in Surveys

A preliminary version is finally available of a survey of the quality of life of men with prostate cancer. The survey team brings 12 patients together to review the survey questionnaire. The focus group moderator asks them a number of specific questions: "Does the questionnaire cover all pertinent topics?" "Can you follow the directions easily?" "How long did it take you to complete the questionnaire?" The survey team will use the results of the focus group's discussion to modify the questionnaire for administration to a large sample of men with prostate cancer.

members of a focus group are different from others in the larger population from which they are drawn in unanticipated ways (e.g., more educated), however, the group's responses may not be applicable to the entire population.

The following table presents descriptions of the most commonly used probability and nonprobability sampling methods and their benefits, as well as some issues you need to resolve when using each method.

Commonly Used Probability
and Nonprobability Sampling Methods

Description	Benefits	Issues
Probability sampling *Simple random sampling* Every unit has an equal chance of selection.	Relatively simple to do.	Members of a subgroup of interest may not be included in appropriate proportions.
Stratified random sampling The study population is grouped according to meaningful characteristics or strata.	Can conduct analyses of subgroups (e.g., men and women; older and younger; East and West). Sampling variations are lower than for random sampling; the sample is more likely to reflect the population.	Must calculate sample sizes for each subgroup. Can be time-consuming and costly to implement if many subgroups are necessary.
Systematic sampling Every Xth unit on a list of eligible units is selected. (Xth can mean 5th, 6th, 23rd, and so on, determined by dividing the size of the population by the desired sample size.)	Convenient; existing list (e.g., of names) used as a sampling frame. Similar to random sampling if starting point (first name chosen) is randomly divided.	Must watch for recurring patterns within the sampling frame (e.g., names beginning with a certain letter, data arranged by month).
Cluster/multistage sampling Natural groups or clusters are sampled, with members of each selected group subsampled afterward.	Convenient; existing units (e.g., schools, hospitals) are used.	

Description	Benefits	Issues
Nonprobability sampling *Convenience sampling* A readily available group of individuals or units is used.	A practical method because it relies on readily available units (e.g., students in a school, patients in a waiting room).	Because sample is opportunistic and voluntary, participants may be unlike most of the constituents in the target population.
Snowball sampling Previously identified members identify other members of the population.	Useful when it is difficult or impractical to obtain a list of names for sampling.	Recommendations may produce a biased sample. Little or no control over who is named.
Quota sampling The population is divided into subgroups (e.g., men and women who are living alone, living with a partner or significant other, not living alone but not living with a partner). A sample is selected based on the proportions of subgroups needed to represent the proportions in the population.	Practical if reliable data exist to describe proportions (e.g., percentage of men over a certain age living alone versus those living with partners).	Records must be up-to-date if you are to get accurate proportions.
Focus groups Groups of 6 to 10 people serve as representatives of a population.	Useful in guiding survey development.	Must be certain the relatively small group is a valid reflection of the larger group that will be surveyed.

2 Statistics and Samples

This chapter covers material that is fairly technical. It is designed to familiarize you with the basic terms and concepts associated with sampling.

Sampling Error

A good sample is an accurately and efficiently assembled model of the population. No matter how proficient you are, however, **sampling error** or **bias** is inevitable. One major source of error in samples arises from procedures and situations outside of the sampling process. This may appear contradictory, but the fact is that such nonsampling error affects the accuracy of a survey's findings because it mars the sample's representativeness. Nonsampling error occurs because of imprecise definitions of the target and study populations and errors in survey design and measurement.

Suppose you plan to conduct a survey to determine the mental health needs of homeless children. One problem you might encounter is that during the time it takes to complete your survey, the children's needs may change because of historical circumstances. New health policies put into effect during the same time period as your survey, for example, could produce programs and services that take care of currently homeless children's most pressing needs. One way of avoiding this type of bias—that is, bias that comes about because of a change in the definition of needs—is to organize the survey so that its duration is not likely to coincide with any major historical changes, such as alterations in policies to improve the availability of mental health services. This requires careful timing and an understanding of the political and social contexts in which all surveys—even small ones—take place.

A second nonsampling problem relates to definitions of variables and terms as well as inclusion and exclusion criteria. For example, a particular survey's definitions of *mental health needs* and *homeless* will necessarily include some children and exclude others. Your definitions of key survey concepts should be based on the best available theory and practice; you might also ask experts to comment on them and on the extent to which they are likely to be applicable to the target population.

Another source of nonsampling bias is nonresponse. Not everyone who is eligible to take part in a survey participates, and not everyone who participates answers all survey questions. You can use a number of methods to improve response rates, such as paying respondents for their participation, sending reminder notices that survey responses are due, and protecting respondents with confidentiality and anonymity.

Biases may also be introduced by the measurement or survey process itself. Poorly worded questions and response choices, inadequately trained interviewers, and unreadable survey questionnaires contribute to the possibility of error.

Sampling error arises from the selection process. A list of names with duplicate entries will favor some people over others, for example. Most typically, selection bias results when nonprobability sampling methods are used and not everyone in the population of interest has a nonzero probability of being chosen. Selection bias is insidious, and it can effectively damage the credibility of your survey.

The best way to avoid selection bias is to use probability sampling methods. If you cannot, you must demonstrate that the target population and the sample do not differ statistically on selected but important variables, such as age, health status, and education. You can get data on these variables from reports on vital statistics (such as those made available by the U.S. Census Bureau and or other federal, state, and local registries) and other published sources. For example, suppose you are conducting a survey of low-income women who have participated in a statewide program to improve their use of prenatal care services. Without comparison data, you have no way of knowing the extent of bias in your sample, although you can be fairly sure some bias is there. If the use of prenatal care services has increased, you cannot be certain that the program was the cause. The women who participated may have been more motivated to seek care to begin with than were nonparticipants. Useful comparison information may be available in the published literature on prenatal care. By examining the literature, you may be able to find out about the patterns of use maintained by women of similar backgrounds.

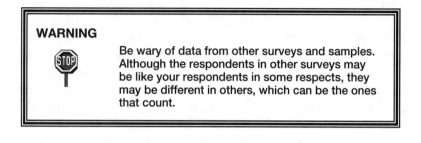

WARNING

Be wary of data from other surveys and samples. Although the respondents in other surveys may be like your respondents in some respects, they may be different in others, which can be the ones that count.

All samples contain errors. Although a sample is chosen to exemplify a target population, chance dictates that the two are unlikely to be identical. When you use probability sampling methods, you can calculate how much a sample varies, by chance, from the population.

If you draw an infinite number of samples from a population, the statistics you produce to describe the sample, such as the mean (the numerical average), standard deviation, or proportion, will form a normal distribution around the population value. (You can find additional information about the mean, standard deviation, proportion, and normal distribution in **How to Manage, Analyze, and Interpret Survey Data**, Volume 9 in this series.) For example, suppose that the mean score in a survey of attitudes toward a bond issue is 50. An examination of an infinite number of means taken from an infinite number of samples would find the means clustering around 50. The means that are computed from each sample form a distribution of values called the **sampling distribution.** When the sample size reaches 30 or more participants, the distribution of the sampling means has the shape of the normal distribution. This is true no matter what the shape of the frequency distribution of the study population is, as long as a large number of samples are selected.

The sample means tend to gather closer around the true population mean with larger samples and less variation in what is being measured. The variation of the sample means around the true value is called **sampling error.** The statistic used to describe the sampling error is called the **standard error of the mean.** The difference between the **standard deviation** and the standard error of the mean is that the standard deviation tells how much variability can be expected among individuals. The standard error of the mean is the standard deviation of the means in a sampling distribution. It tells how much variability can be expected among means in future samples.

When the value of a standard error has been estimated, 68% of the means of samples of a given size and design will fall within the range of 1 standard error of the true population mean; 95% of the samples will fall within 2 standard errors. This is shown in Figure 2.1. When you report your survey results, you present them in terms of how confident you are that the samples fall within the range of 2 standard errors.

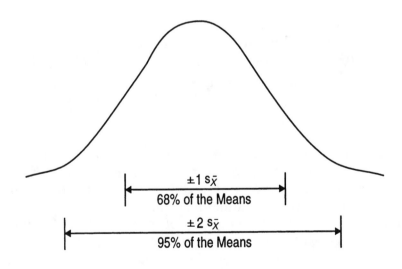

Figure 2.1.   Sampling Distribution of the Mean

ESTIMATING THE STANDARD ERROR
FOR SIMPLE RANDOM SAMPLES

Although a basic understanding of statistical notation will be helpful to you in reading the material that follows, even if you are "nontechnically oriented," you should plow through to the extent possible because of the importance of the logic and principles of sampling that are discussed. Sampling is a complicated activity, and you should seek the advice of experts in undertaking it. However, you will find that consultation with experts is always more satisfying and efficient if you understand the vocabulary and the principles they are using.

The formula for estimating the standard error of a mean is calculated from the variance and the size of the sample from which it was estimated:

$$SE = \sqrt{Var / n}$$

where

$$\sqrt{} = \text{square root}$$
$$SE = \text{standard error of the mean,}$$
$$Var = \text{variance (sum of the squared deviations}$$
$$\text{from the sample mean over } n)$$
$$n = \text{number of individuals comprising the sample}$$

Surveyors typically report proportions or percentages of respondents answering yes or no. For example, 20% of the respondents said yes when asked if they understand the difference between the standard deviation and the standard error, and 80% said no. One way of thinking about the proportion is as the mean of a two-value distribution.

The mean is the average. The formula for calculating the sample mean is

$$\bar{X} = \sum X / n$$

where
$$\bar{X} \quad = \quad \text{mean (numerical average)}$$
- = sum of (represented by the uppercase Greek letter sigma)

X = number of observations (e.g., number of people answering yes)

n = sample size (e.g., number of people who answered the question)

Suppose you have two values: 1 = yes and 0 = no. You have 100 people in the sample, and 20 say yes and 80 say no. The mean of the two values—20 and 80—can be calculated this way:

$$\sum X = (20 \times 1) + (80 \times 0) = 20$$

$$\sum X / n = 20 / 100 = .20$$

A proportion or percentage (e.g., 20% said that they do not understand the difference between standard deviations and errors) is a statement about the mean of a 1/0 distribution, and the mean is .20.

The formula for calculating the standard error of a proportion includes the following:

$$p(1-p)$$

where

p = proportion with the characteristic (e.g., 20% yes)

$1-p$ = proportion without the characteristic (e.g., 80% no)

To calculate the standard error of a proportion, start with the formula for the standard error of the mean ($\sqrt{\text{Var}/n}$). The variation for the proportion is $p(1 - p)$, and so the formula for the standard error of a proportion becomes

$$\sqrt{p(1 \pm p) / n}$$

With 20% of a 100-person sample understanding the difference between standard deviations and standard errors, the standard error would be

$$\sqrt{p(1 \pm p)/n} = \sqrt{(.20 \times .80)/100} = \sqrt{.16/100} = .04$$

If you add .04 to the yes vote and also subtract .04 from it, you have an interval from .24 to .16. You can say that the probability is .68 (1 standard error from the sample mean) that the true population figure is within that interval. If you want to be 95% confident, then you must add 2 standard errors, and the interval now becomes .28 to .12. You can now say that you are 95% confident that the true population mean is between .28 and .12.

Example 2.1 illustrates how you can use a table to arrive at the estimated sampling error for a percentage of a sample that has a certain "binomial" characteristic (under 19 years of age or over; male or female) or provides a certain response (yes or no; agree or not agree). You use such a table by finding the connection between the sample size and the approximate percentage for each characteristic or response. The number appearing at the connection is the estimated sampling error at the 95% confidence level.

EXAMPLE 2.1
How to Establish Confidence Intervals

In a survey of 100 respondents, 70% answer yes and 30% answer no to a particular question. According to the following table, the sampling error is ±9.2 percentage points. Adding 9.2 and subtracting 9.2 from the 70% who say yes, you get a confidence interval between 79.2% and 60.8%. You can estimate with 95% confidence that the proportion of the sample saying yes is somewhere in the interval.

Example 2.1 continued

Sample Size	Binomial (yes, no; on, off) Percentage Distribution				
	50/50	60/40	70/30	80/20	90/10
100	10	9.8	9.2	8	6
200	7.1	6.9	6.5	5.7	4.2
300	5.8	5.7	5.3	4.6	3.5
400	5	4.9	4.6	4	3
500	4.5	4.4	4.1	3.6	2.7
600	4.1	4	3.7	3.3	2.4
700	3.8	3.7	3.5	3	2.3
800	3.5	3.5	3.3	2.8	2.1
900	3.3	3.3	3.1	2.7	2
1,000	3.2	3.1	3	2.5	1.9
1,100	3	3	2.8	2.4	1.8
1,200	2.9	2.8	2.6	2.3	1.7
1,300	2.8	2.7	2.5	2.2	1.7
1,400	2.7	2.6	2.4	2.1	1.6
1,500	2.6	2.5	2.4	2.1	1.5
1,600	2.5	2.4	2.3	2	1.5
1,700	2.4	2.4	2.2	1.9	1.4
1,800	2.4	2.3	2.2	1.9	1.4
1,900	2.3	2.2	2.1	1.8	1.3
2,000	2.2	2.2	2	1.8	1.3

Remember that the table applies only to errors due to sampling. Other sources of error, such as nonsampling errors or nonresponse, are not reflected in this table. Also, the table works only for simple random samples. For other sampling methods and confidence levels, a more advanced knowledge of statistics is required than is assumed here.

EXERCISES

1. In a survey of 200 respondents, 60% say yes to a particular question. What is the confidence interval for a 95% confidence level?

2. In a survey of 150 respondents, 90% say yes to a particular question. What is the confidence interval for a 95% confidence level?

• •
ANSWERS

1. 53.1% to 69.8% (interval of 9.8%)

2. About 85% to 95% (interval of about 5%)

Sample Size: How Much Is Enough?

The size of the sample is the numbers of units that need to be surveyed in order for the findings to be precise and reliable. The units can be people (e.g., men and women over and under 45 years of age), places (e.g., counties, hospitals, schools), or things (e.g., medical or school records).

The influence of increasing sample size on sampling variation or standard error is shown in Figure 2.2, which illustrates how sampling variability decreases as sample size increases. The gain in precision is greater for each unit increase in the smaller sample size range than in the larger.

When you increase the sample's size, you increase the survey's costs. Larger samples mean increased costs for data collection (especially for interviews), data processing, and

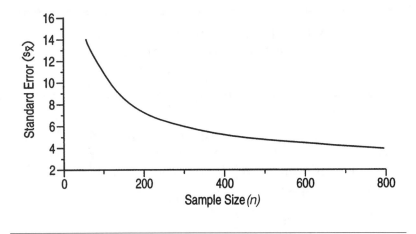

Figure 2.2.   Sample Size and Sample Variation

analysis. Moreover, increasing the sample size may divert attention from other sampling activities, such as following up with eligible people who fail to respond, and this may actually increase total sampling error. It is very important to remember that many factors affect the amount of error or chance variation in the sample. Aside from nonresponse, one of these is the design of a sample. If the sample design deviates from simple random sampling, relies on cluster sampling, or does not use probability sampling, the total error will invariably decrease the quality of the survey's findings. The size of the sample, although a leading contender in the sampling error arena, is just one of several factors you need to consider in coming up with a "good" sample.

The most appropriate way to determine the right sample size is through the use of statistical calculations. These can be relatively complex, depending on the needs of the survey. Some surveys have just one sample, and others have several. Like most survey activities, sample size considerations should be placed within a broad context. You may find the following checklist of factors to account for useful when you are attempting to determine the proper sample size for your survey.

Checklist of Factors to Consider
When Calculating Sample Size

✓ Assemble and clarify all survey objectives, questions, or hypotheses.

Before you begin to consider the size of the sample, you must decide on the objectives, questions, or hypotheses your survey is to answer. Consider the following examples:

- Survey 1: Quality of Life

  Objective: To determine whether younger and older women differ in their quality of life after surgery for breast cancer

  Question: Do younger and older women differ in their quality of life after surgery for breast cancer?

  Hypothesis: Younger and older women do not differ in their quality of life after surgery for breast cancer.

- Survey 2: Fear in School

  Objective: To determine whether students in urban schools are more fearful of violence or of tests

  Question: Which do students in urban schools fear more: violence or tests?

  Hypothesis: Students in urban schools fear violence more than they fear tests.

- Survey 3: Use of Mental Health Services

  Objective: To determine which of a number of listed circumstances account for ethnic/racial differences in the use of mental health services

Question: Which of the listed circumstances account for ethnic/racial differences in the use of mental health services?

Hypothesis: Lack of knowledge regarding where to go for services predicts underuse of services among African Americans.

- Survey 4: Attitude Toward Dieting and Exercising

Objective: To determine whether there are differences in attitudes toward dieting and exercising and knowledge of health among men and women of differing ages after participation in the company's new and traditional health-promotion/risk-reduction programs

Question: Are there differences in attitudes toward dieting and exercising and knowledge of health among men and women of differing ages after participation in the company's new and traditional health-promotion/risk-reduction programs?

Hypothesis: After participation in the company's new and traditional health-promotion/risk-reduction programs, men and women of differing ages show differences in attitudes toward dieting and exercising but not in knowledge of health.

The objectives, questions, and hypotheses presented above are only illustrations, and there are few differences in how they are stated. You should be aware, however, that hypotheses require special handling; this is discussed later.

Each objective, question, and hypothesis contains the survey's independent and dependent variables.

Independent variables, the "grouping variables," are used to predict or explain the dependent variables. Take the question "Do boys and girls differ in their attitudes toward school?" The grouping or independent variable is gender. The hidden question is whether one can predict attitudes based on knowledge of gender. In statistical terms, the independent variables specify the conditions under which estimates of or inferences about the dependent variable are to be made.

Dependent variables are the attitudes, behaviors, and knowledge the survey is measuring. In statistical terms, they are the variables for which estimates are to be made or inferences drawn. In the question "Do boys and girls differ in their attitudes toward school?" the dependent variable is attitudes toward school.

Independent and dependent variables can be divided into categories or levels. Gender has two categories: male and female. The following table displays the independent and dependent variables of the four surveys above.

	Independent Variable	**Dependent Variable**
Survey 1	Age of women (older and younger)	Quality of life
Survey 2	Students in urban schools	Fear: of violence and tests
Survey 3	Ethnic/racial groups (e.g., African American, Latino, White, Asian Pacific Islander, Chinese, Japanese)	Use of mental health services
Survey 4	Health-promotion programs (new and traditional), gender (male and female), age (youngest to oldest employee)	Attitude toward dieting and exercising; knowledge of the effects of diet and exercise

✓ Identify subgroups.

You need to identify the subgroups in the sample from which you must collect sufficient data to arrive at accurate conclusions. You can identify the subgroups in the four surveys above, for example, by looking at the independent variables. Survey 1's subgroups are older and younger women, Survey 3's are ethnic and racial groups (e.g., African American, Latino), and Survey 4's are new and traditional programs, males and females, and youngest to oldest employees. Survey 2 does not specify subgroups.

✓ Identify survey type and data collection needs.

The dependent variables signal the content of the survey. For example, Survey 1's questions will ask respondents about various aspects of their quality of life, Survey 2's will ask about fear in school, Survey 3's about use of mental health services, and Survey 4's about attitudes toward diet and exercise and knowledge of health. For illustrative purposes, assume that Surveys 1 and 4 are in-person interviews, Survey 2 is a self-administered questionnaire, and Survey 3 is a telephone interview.

Interviews and self-administered questionnaires have specific and general data collection needs. The specific needs vary according to the survey's situation. For example, the survey about use of mental health services may need to be translated into more than one language, and the survey about fear in school may need to be anonymous. General data collection needs are those that are inherent in the survey method itself. For instance, face-to-face interviews require extensive interviewer training and are labor-intensive. With mailed questionnaires, although the initial costs of paper and postage may be low, the costs of follow-up and nonresponse may be high.

✓ Check the survey's resources and schedule.

Surveys that have many subgroups and measures are more complex and more costly to conduct than those with fewer subgroups and measures. Consider Example 2.2.

Example 2.3 presents a sampling blueprint of Survey 4 that illustrates how complex a survey with many subgroups can be. This survey has 12 subgroups: new program, traditional program, men of five ages, and women of five ages.

A sampling blueprint provides a pictorial representation of the sampling plan. The blueprint in Example 2.3 is a picture of the groups that are to be surveyed in order to answer the question "Are there differences in attitudes toward dieting and exercising and knowledge of health among men and women of differing ages [defined in the blueprint as 20-25, 26-30, 31-40, 41-55, and over 55] after participation in the company's new and traditional health-promotion/risk-reduction programs?"

Each of the subgroups is represented in the blueprint by an empty box, or *cell*. Three subgroups are marked by asterisks as examples. To achieve this configuration of subgroups, you can use stratified random sampling. If you are comparing attitudes after participation in the new and traditional programs, a statistical rule of thumb suggests that you need about 30 people in each group. If you increase the number of cells or subgroups, you also need to increase the sample's size so that you have at least 30 in each subgroup. This is shown in the two hypothetical cases displayed in Example 2.4. In Case 1,

EXAMPLE 2.2
Subgroups, Measures,
Resources, and Schedule

	Subgroups	Type of Survey	Comments
Survey 1: Do younger and older women differ in their quality of life after surgery for breast cancer?	Younger and older women: 2 subgroups	In-person interview	May need time to hire and train different interviewers for younger and older women May have difficulty recruiting sufficient numbers of eligible younger or older women
Survey 2: Are students in urban schools more fearful of violence or of tests?	Students in urban schools: 1 group	Self-administered questionnaire	May need time to translate the questionnaire from English into other languages Must decide whether to make survey confidential or anonymous
Survey 3: Which of the listed circumstances account for ethnic/racial differences in the use of mental health services?	Race/ethnicity: African American, White, Latino, Chinese, Japanese, Southeast Asian, Asian Pacific Islander: 7 subgroups	Telephone interview	May need time to hire and train interviewers who speak many languages
Survey 4: Are there differences in attitudes toward dieting and exercising and knowledge of health among men and women of differing ages after participation in the company's new and traditional health-promotion/risk-reduction programs?	Men and women of five differing ages; new and traditional programs: 12 subgroups	In-person interview	Will have to administer one survey with both knowledge and attitude components or two separate surveys May need time to find or develop the survey

EXAMPLE 2.3
Sampling Blueprint

	New Program		Traditional Program	
Years of Age	Men	Women	Men	Women
20-25		*		*
26-30				
31-40				
41-55				
Over 55	*			

NOTE: The asterisks (*) are guides for reading the blueprint. They represent women between 20 and 25 in the new program, women between 20 and 25 in the traditional program, and men over 55 in the new program.

EXAMPLE 2.4
More Subgroups and Larger Samples

Case 1

New Program	Traditional Program	Total
Sample = 30	Sample = 30	Sample = 60

Case 2

New Program		Traditional Program		
Men	Women	Men	Women	Total
Sample = 30	Sample = 30	Sample = 30	Sample = 30	Sample = 120

the new and traditional programs are compared, and 60 people are needed. In Case 2, men and women are compared in each program, and 120 people are needed.

Large numbers of subgroups and measures increase the costs of a survey and the time needed to complete it. If your resources and the time you have available are incompatible with your survey aspirations, you will need to find a compromise.

Calculating Sample Size

The ideal sample is a miniature version of the target population. To achieve this ideal, you must use techniques that will help you to avoid biases due to nonsampling and design errors. Nonsampling errors arise from poor definitions of the target and nonresponse. Design errors occur when sample selection deviates from probability techniques. The ideal sample is also large enough that it allows you to detect effects or changes. Several different formulas are available for use in estimating sample sizes; in fact, a number of books are devoted to the subject.

Suppose a survey is concerned with finding out whether a program is effective in improving the health, education, and quality of life of adolescents. Assume also that one survey objective is to compare the goals and aspirations of adolescents in the program with adolescents who are not in the program. How large should each group of adolescents be? To answer this question, you first need to answer the five questions posed in the following checklist.

Checklist of Questions to Ask
When Determining Sample Size

✓ What is the null hypothesis?

The **null hypothesis** (H_0) is a statement that no difference exists between the average or mean scores of two groups. For example, one null hypothesis for the survey of adolescents is that no difference exists between adolescents participating in the program and nonparticipants in terms of their goals and aspirations (as measured by average survey scores).

✓ What is the desired level of significance (? level) related to the null hypothesis involving the mean in the population (μ_0)?

NOTE: In hypothesis testing, the mean in the population (represented by μ, the Greek letter mu) is used rather than the mean in the sample ($\overline{X}$).

The **level of significance**, when chosen before the test is performed, is called the **alpha value** (denoted by α, the Greek letter alpha). The alpha value gives the probability of rejecting the null hypothesis when it is actually true. Tradition keeps the alpha value small—.05, .01, or .001—to avoid the rejection of a null hypothesis when it is true (and no difference exists between group means). The **p value** is the probability that an observed result (or result of a statistical test) is due to chance (rather than to participation in a program). It is calculated *after* the statistical test. If the p value is less than alpha, the null is rejected.

✓ What chance should there be of detecting an actual difference? Put another way, what is the power ($1 - \beta$, or Greek letter beta) associated with the alternative hypothesis involving μ_1?

When differences are found to exist between two groups although in reality there are no differences, that is called an alpha error or **Type I error**. When no differences are found between groups even though in reality there are differences, that is termed a beta error or **Type II error**. These relationships are shown in the following table.

	Truth	
	Differences Exist	**No Differences Exist**
Differences exist (reject null)	Correct	Type I or alpha error
No differences exist (keep null)	Type II or beta error	Correct

✓ What degree of difference between the means must be detected for the difference to be important? That is, what is a meaningful $\mu_1 - \mu_2$?

Suppose the survey uses the Goals and Aspirations Scale, a hypothetical scale that has 50 points. The first step in the use of this scale (or any other survey searching for differences) is to decide on a difference between means that is important in practical and statistical terms. To make this decision, you can seek expert guidance and ask questions like "Will a 5-point difference matter? Will a 10-point difference matter?" (This difference is sometimes referred to as the *effect,* and the size of the difference is the **effect size**.)

✓ What is a good estimate of the standard deviation σ
in the population?

The **standard deviation** (denoted by σ, lowercase
Greek letter sigma) is a common measure of the dispersion or spread of the data around the mean. Two general
rules apply to the standard deviation. First, at least 75%
of all values (such as scores) always lie between the mean
and 2 standard deviations. If 100 people complete a survey and their mean score is 25 and the standard deviation is 2, then at least 75 respondents will have scores of
25 ± 4. That is, their scores will fall between 21 and 29.

If the distribution of values or observations is a bell-
shaped or normal distribution, then 68% of the observations will fall between the mean ±1 standard deviation,
95% will fall between ±2 standard deviations, and 99%
will fall between ±3 standard deviations.

You can get an estimate of the standard deviation
from a previously conducted survey, but before you use
it, be sure to check that the earlier survey's population is
similar to your own. If not, the standard deviation is also
likely to be different. Alternatively, you can conduct a
small pilot test using about 25 people and calculate the
standard deviation. Or you can use experts' estimates of
the highest and lowest values or scores as the basis for
calculating the standard deviation.

The formula for calculating sample size for comparing
the means from two independent groups (e.g., adolescents participating in a program to improve their health
and education versus nonparticipants) is given below.
This is one of many formulas you might use in calculating sample size for surveys; the aim of all such formulas
is to determine how many survey respondents are
needed to produce accurate findings. This formula
assumes that the standard deviations in the two populations are equal and that the sample sizes are equal in the
two groups:

$$\frac{\left(Z_\alpha - Z_\beta\right)\sigma^2}{\mu_1 \pm \mu_2}$$

where

$\mu_1 - \mu_2$ = the magnitude of the difference to be detected between the two groups

Z_α = the upper tail in the normal distribution

Z_β = the lower tail in the normal distribution).

These "tails" are defined as

$$Z_\alpha = \frac{X \pm \mu_1}{\sigma/\sqrt{n}} \text{ and } Z_\beta = \frac{X \pm \mu_2}{\sigma/\sqrt{n}}$$

Example 2.5 illustrates the application of the formula.

EXAMPLE 2.5
Calculating Sample Size in a Survey of Adolescents in Experimental and Control Groups

Survey Situation

Two groups of adolescents are participating in a program to improve their health, education, and quality of life. At the conclusion of the 3-year program, participants in the experimental and control groups will be surveyed to find out about their goals and aspirations. The highest score on the survey is 100 points. The Type I

Example 2.5 continued

error or alpha level is set at .05. The probability of detecting a true difference is set at .80. Experts in adolescent behavior say that the difference in scores between the experimental and control groups (the size of the effect) should be 10 points or more. Previous experiments using the survey have revealed a standard deviation of 15 points.

Calculations

For the calculation, let us assume that a standard normal distribution, or *z* distribution, is appropriate. The standard normal curve has a mean of 0 and a standard deviation of 1. The two-tailed *z* value related to $\alpha = .05$ is 1.96 (for more about the standard normal distribution, one- and two-tailed tests, and *z* values, see **How to Manage, Analyze, and Interpret Survey Data**, Volume 9 in this series; actual *z* values are obtainable in any elementary statistics book). For $\alpha = .01$, the two-tailed *z* value is 2.58; for $\alpha = .10$, 1.65; and for $\alpha = .20$, 1.28. The lower one-tailed *z* value related to β is $- .84$ (the critical value or *z* score separating the lower 20% of the *z* distribution from 80%). Applying the formula

$$(1.96 + 0.84)(15)^2 = 2\left(\frac{42}{10}\right)^2$$

$$= 2 (17.64), \text{ or about } 36$$

At least 36 adolescents are needed in each group in order for the survey to have an 80% chance of detecting a difference in scores of 10 points.

HELP WITH SAMPLE SIZE AND POWER

Choosing a sample and determining how big it must be to have sufficient power to detect differences are not for novices. An excellent resource for help with decisions on sample size is available free on the Internet (at www.mc.vanderbilt.edu/prevmed/ps/index.htm), thanks to Vanderbilt University and two researchers: William Dupont and Walton Plummer, Jr. They describe their program for calculating power and sample size, *PS*, as follows:

PS is an interactive program for performing power and sample size calculations. The program runs on the Windows 95, Windows 98, Windows NT, and Windows 2000 operating systems. It can be used for studies with dichotomous, continuous, or survival response measures. The alternative hypothesis of interest may be specified either in terms of differing response rates, means, or survival times, or in terms of relative risks or odds ratios. Studies with dichotomous or continuous outcomes may involve either a matched or independent study design. The program can determine the sample size needed to detect a specified alternative hypothesis with the required power, the power with which a specific alternative hypothesis can be detected with a given sample size, or the specific alternative hypotheses that can be detected with a given power and sample size.

The *PS* program can produce graphs to explore the relationships between power, sample size, and detectable alternative hypotheses. It is often helpful to hold one of these variables constant and plot the other two against each other. The program can generate graphs of sample size versus power for a specific alternative hypothesis, sample size versus detectable alternative hypotheses for a specified power, or power versus detectable alternative hypotheses for a specified sample size. Linear or logarithmic axes may be used for either axes. Multiple curves can be plotted on a single graphic.

Many step-by-step guides are available on the Web to guide you through the process of calculating sample size and power. Two of these can be found at ebook.stat.ucla.edu and www.surveysystem.com. If all else fails, you can enter the keywords *sample* and *size* into any online search engine, and you will be led to many more resources.

Sampling Units and the Unit of Analysis

A **sampling unit** is an individual, group, or other entity that is selected for the survey or assigned to groups. The **unit of analysis** is the entity whose survey data are examined statistically. Sometimes, the sampling and analysis units are the same, as in simple one-stage sampling. In more complex multistage samples, the sampling and analysis units are not the same. The differences are illustrated in Example 2.6.

EXAMPLE 2.6
Sampling Unit and Unit of Analysis:
Sometimes the Same and Sometimes Not

Case 1: Sampling Unit and Unit of Analysis
Are the Same

Survey Objective: To determine if the program ENHANCE has improved students' attitudes toward school

Sampling Method: Names of 500 eligible students are compiled from school records. From the list, 200 names are randomly selected. Of these, 100 students are randomly assigned to the experimental program and 100 are assigned to the control program.

Example 2.6 continued

Survey Instrument: A 10-item self-administered question-naire. A positive answer to a question means a favorable response.

Statistical Analysis: The number of positive answers on each questionnaire is added to come up with a score. The average scores in the experimental and control groups are computed. A comparison is made between the two groups' average scores to test for statistical differences.

Sampling Unit: The student (individual students are selected; individual students are assigned)

Unit of Analysis: The student (each student's question-naire is scored, and the scores are aggregated and averaged across students)

Case 2: Sampling Unit and Unit of Analysis Are Different

Survey Objective: To determine if the program ENHANCE has improved students' attitudes toward school

Sampling Method: Four elementary schools are selected because they represent the district's 14 schools in terms of enrollment size and family demographics (e.g., socioeconomic indicators). The four schools are grouped into two pairs, AB and CD. A 30% sample of second-grade classrooms (16 classrooms totaling 430 students) in the first members of the two pairs of schools is selected at random from the total second-grade enrollment to receive the experimental program in the first semester. A 20% random sample of second-grade classrooms (10 classrooms totaling 251 students) in the second members of

Example 2.6 continued

the two pairs serves as the comparison or control group (receiving no formal program). Similarly, a 30% sample of fourth-grade classrooms (13 classrooms totaling 309 students) in the second members of the two pairs of schools is selected at random from the total fourth-grade enrollment to receive the special program curriculum in the first semester, and a 20% random sample of the fourth-grade enrollment (13 classrooms totaling 326 students) in the first members of the two pairs serves as the control. Of the 1,316 students participating, 739 students are assigned to the experimental program and 577 to the control. The sampling strategy provides a greater than 80% power to detect a "small" treatment difference, holding a Type I error at 5%. The sampling strategy can be graphically illustrated as follows:

	Experimental Group		Control Group	
Schools	AB	CD	AB	CD
Grade	2	4	4	2
Semester	First	Second	Second	First
% Sample	30	30	20	20
Number of Classrooms	16	13	13	10
Number of Students	430	309	326	251
Sample size				
Classrooms	29		23	
Students	739		577	

Example 2.6 continued

Survey Instrument: A 10-item self-administered question-naire. A positive answer to a question means a favorable response.

Statistical Analysis: The number of positive answers on each questionnaire is added to come up with a score. The average scores in the experimental and control groups are computed. A comparison is made between the two groups' average scores to test for statistical differences.

Sampling Units: The school and the classroom (schools are selected; classrooms are selected and assigned)

Unit of Analysis: The student (each student's question-naire is scored, and the scores are aggregated across students)

The small number of schools and classrooms in the survey in Case 2 in the example precludes their use as the unit of statistical analysis: Larger samples are needed to detect any existing differences. However, the number of students provides a sample with power greater than 80% to detect a "small" treatment difference, holding a Type I error at 5%.

The sampling method described in Case 2 has several potential biases. First, the small numbers of schools and classrooms may result in initial differences that may strongly influence the outcome of the program. Second, students in each school or classroom may perform as a unit primarily because they have the same teacher or were placed in the classroom because of their similar abilities or interests.

When your survey's unit of analysis is different from the sampling unit, you will often be called on to demonstrate statistically or logically that your results are similar to those that would have been obtained had both units been the same. If the analysis finds initial group differences in baseline levels and demographic factors, for example, you may be able to use statistical methods to "adjust" program effects in view of the differences (for more information on such statistical methods, see **How to Manage, Analyze, and Interpret Survey Data**, Volume 9 in this series).

Acceptable Response Rate

All survey researchers hope for high **response rates**. No single rate is considered the standard, however. In some surveys, rates of between 95% and 100% are expected; in others, rates of 70% are considered to be adequate.

Consider the five cases in Example 2.7. In Case 1, 5% of eligible state residents do not complete the interview. These nonrespondents may be very different from the 95% who do respond in their health needs, incomes, and education. When nonrespondents and respondents differ on important factors, *nonresponse bias* is introduced. In Case 1, the relatively high response rate of 95% suggests that the respondents are probably similar to most of the state's residents in the distribution of health problems and demographics. Very high response rates in interview surveys often are the result of time invested by the survey team in the training of interviewers; this includes opportunities to provide interviewers with feedback and retraining, if needed.

EXAMPLE 2.7
Five Cases and Five Response Rates

1. The National State Health Interview is completed by a 95% sample of all who are eligible. Health officials conclude that the 5%

Example 2.7 continued

who do not participate probably differ from participants in their health needs and demographic characteristics. They also decide that the 95% who respond are representative of most of the state's population.

2. According to statistical calculations, the Commission on Refugee Affairs needs a sample of 100 for its mail survey. Based on the results of previous mailings, the survey team anticipates a refusal rate of 20% to 25%, so, to allow for this possibility, the commission sends the survey to 125 eligible people.

3. A sample of employees at Uniting Airlines participate in interviews regarding their job satisfaction. A 100% response is achieved.

4. A sample of recent travelers on Uniting Airlines are sent a mail survey. After the first mailing, a 20% response rate is achieved.

5. Parents of children attending an elementary school are mailed a questionnaire about their knowledge of injury prevention for children. Each parent who sends in a completed questionnaire receives a cash payment within 2 weeks. To receive the payment, the parent must complete all 25 questions on the survey. An 85% response rate is obtained.

Practically all surveys suffer some loss of information due to nonresponse. The survey team in Case 2 uses past information to estimate the probable response rate and decides to *oversample* in the hope that this will result in responses from the desired number of respondents. Oversampling can add costs to a survey, but it is often necessary. To determine how much oversampling you may need to do, you should try to anticipate the proportion of people who, although otherwise apparently eligible, may not turn up in the sample. In mail surveys, for example, this can happen if addresses are out-of-date and the questionnaires are undeliverable. It is very frustrating and costly to send out a survey only to find that half of the addressees have moved. With telephone interviews, respondents may not be at home. Sometimes, people cannot be interviewed in person because they suddenly become ill.

In Case 3 in Example 2.7, a 100% response rate is obtained. Response rates are always highest if the topic is of interest to the respondents or if completion of a survey is considered to be part of employees' obligation to participate in information management.

Unsolicited surveys receive the lowest response rates. A 20% response for a first mailing, as in Case 4, is not uncommon. With effort, response rates on such surveys can be elevated to 70% or even 80%. Follow-up mailings and the use of graphically sophisticated surveys can improve response rates, as can incentives for respondents such as monetary payments and small gifts (pens, books, radios, audio- and videocassettes, and so on). In some situations, as in Case 4, the adequacy of the response rates can be calculated within a range, say, of 70% to 75%.

In Case 5, the respondents are paid upon completion of all questions and return of the survey, and a relatively high response rate of 85% is achieved. Incentives of cash or gifts will succeed in promoting a high return rate only if the respondents who are contacted are available and able to complete the survey.

Nonresponse to an entire survey introduces error or bias. Another type of nonresponse can also introduce bias: item nonresponse. Item nonresponse occurs when a respondent or survey administrator does not complete all items on a survey form. This type of bias comes about when respondents do not know the answers to certain questions or refuse to answer them because they believe them to be sensitive, embarrassing, or irrelevant. Interviewers may skip questions or fail to record answers. In some cases, respondents provide answers that are later rejected because they appear to make no sense. This can happen if a respondent misreads a question or fails to record all the information called for. For example, a respondent may leave out his or her year of birth and record only the month and day.

Survey researchers sometimes use statistical methods to "correct" for nonresponse, whether to the entire survey or just some items. One method is *weighting.* Suppose a surveyor wants to compare younger (under 25 years of age) and older (26 and older) college students' career goals. A review of school records reveals that younger students constitute 40% of the population, but only 20% of younger students sampled return their questionnaires. Using statistical methods, the surveyor can weight the 20% response rate to become the equivalent of 40%. The accuracy of the result depends on how similar the younger respondents are to the younger nonrespondents in their answers and on how different the younger respondents' answers are from those of the older respondents.

Another method of correcting for nonresponse is called *imputation.* A surveyor using this method assigns, or imputes, values for missing responses, using respondents' answers to other items as supplementary information.

Following the guidelines listed below can help you to promote good response rates, minimize response bias, and reduce survey error.

Guidelines for Promoting Responses and Minimizing Response Bias

✓ Use trained interviewers. Set up a quality assurance system to monitor interviewer quality and provide retraining as needed.

✓ Identify a larger number of eligible respondents than you need in case you do not get the sample size you need. Be careful to pay attention to the costs.

✓ Use a survey only when you are fairly certain that potential respondents are interested in the topic.

✓ Keep survey responses confidential or anonymous.

✓ Send the recipients of mail surveys reminders to complete the questionnaire; make repeat phone calls to potential telephone survey respondents.

✓ Provide gift or cash incentives to respondents.

✓ Be realistic about your survey eligibility criteria. Anticipate the proportion of respondents who may not be able to participate because of circumstances (e.g., incorrect addresses) or by chance (e.g., they suddenly become ill).

The response rate is the number of persons who respond (numerator) divided by the number of eligible respondents (denominator):

Response rate = Respondents/Eligible to respond.

Example 2.8 shows how to calculate the response rate.

EXAMPLE 2.8
Calculating the Response Rate

A survey is mailed to 500 women as part of a study to examine the use of screening mammograms in a large health plan. The following eligibility criteria are set:

Inclusion Criteria:

- Over 40 years of age
- Current practice restricts routine screening mammograms to women over 40
- Visited physician in the past year

If a woman visited her doctor in the past year, the survey team will have access to a relatively recent mailing address for her.

- Can read and answer all questions by herself

Exclusion Criteria:

- Does not speak English or Spanish

Nearly all women in the health plan speak English or Spanish, and the researchers do not have the resources to translate the survey into other languages.

- Diagnosed with dementing illness

This is a mail survey. The survey team is unwilling to use "proxies," that is, persons who answer for respondents who cannot answer for themselves, and proxies may be necessary for many people with dementing illnesses (unless mild). Application of this criterion reduces the complexity of the survey.

- Hospitalized for major physical or mental disorder at the time of the survey

This criterion is set to avoid the problem of undeliverable mail.

The first mailing produces responses from 178 women, for a response rate of 35.6% (178/500). After the second mailing, 283 additional women respond, for a total of 461. The survey's response rate is thus 92.2% (461/500).

Exercises

1. Name the sampling method used in each of these four scenarios.

   a. Two of four software companies are chosen to participate in a new work-at-home program. The five department heads in each of the two companies are interviewed. Six employees are selected at random to complete a self-administered questionnaire by electronic mail.

   b. Each of the rangers surveyed at five national parks is asked to recommend two other rangers to participate.

   c. To be eligible to participate in a particular survey, students must attend a local high school and speak English. Students with poor attendance records will be excluded. All remaining students will be surveyed.

   d. The names of all teens who have been incarcerated in a particular county within the past 6 months will be written individually on pieces of paper that will then be placed in a glass jar. A blind-folded referee will select 10 slips of paper from the jar; those whose names appear on the slips will serve on a focus group.

2. Draw a sampling blueprint for a survey whose objective is to answer this question:

> How do employees at five companies compare this year and last year in their preferences for work schedules?

3. Review these three sampling plans and comment on the sources of error or bias.

    a. A self-administered survey to evaluate the quality of medical care is completed by the first 100 patients who seek pre-ventive care. The objective is to find out whether the patients are satisfied with the advice and education given to them. The survey team analyzes the results to identify whether any observed differ-ences can be explained by gender, edu-cation, or health status.

    b. A questionnaire is mailed to all members of Immunity International. About 60% of those who received the question-naires completed and returned them. Immunity is pleased with the return rate because unsolicited mail surveys rarely receive more than 50% returns on the first try.

    c. Two groups of children are interviewed about their television viewing habits.

The children in the two groups have been involved in two different programs to encourage selective TV viewing. One of the programs requires more involvement than the other, and it lasts longer also. Are the two programs equally effective? The plan is to interview at least 100 children in each group, for a total of 200 children. The survey team chose these numbers because a similar program surveyed 200 children and got a very high degree of cooperation.

ANSWERS

EXERCISE 1

1a. Multistage or cluster sampling

1b. Snowball sampling

1c. No sampling (All eligible students—that is, the entire population—will be surveyed.)

1d. Random sampling

EXERCISE 2

Sampling blueprint:

Companies	This Year	Last Year
1		
2		
3		
4		
5		

Exercise 3

3a. This survey of patients' opinions about their medical care uses a convenience sample. Convenience samples are sometimes composed of people who are markedly different from the target population.

3b. Sampling error is a combination of nonsampling and sampling problems. In this case, the error is a nonsampling error caused by a relatively low return rate (although 60% may be high for unsolicited mail surveys without follow-ups). Two-fifths (40%) of those surveyed did not respond.

3c. To ensure the appropriateness of the sample size of 100 children in each of two groups that has been decided upon, based on the sample size of a previous survey, the survey team should ask questions like the following: How much of a difference between groups is required? What is the desired level of significance related to the null hypothesis? What chance should there be of detecting a true difference (power)? What is the standard deviation in the population? It is possible that the previous survey might serve as a guide to the selection of a sample size for the present survey, but the surveyors should not automatically assume that the two are identical with respect to their objectives or expectations.

Suggested Readings

American Association of Public Opinion Research. (2000). *Standard definitions: Final dispositions of case codes and outcome rates for RDD telephone surveys and in-person household surveys.* Ann Arbor, MI: Author.

> *Contains standard definitions for calculating response rates. For a copy of the report, contact AAPOR, P.O. Box 1248, Ann Arbor, MI 48106-1248; telephone (734) 764-1555; fax (734) 764-3341; e-mail aapor@umich.edu; Web site www.aapor.org.*

Babbie, E. (1990). *Survey research methods.* Belmont, CA: Wadsworth.

> *Basic survey research primer with examples of sampling in practice.*

Baker, T. L. (1988). *Doing social research.* New York: McGraw-Hill.

> *A "how-to," with examples.*

Burnham, M. A., & Koegel, P. (1988). Methodology for obtaining a representative sample of homeless persons: The Los Angeles skid row study. *Evaluation Review, 12,* 117-152.

> *Provides an excellent description of how to obtain a representative sample of an elusive population.*

Campbell, D. T., & Stanley, J. C. (1963). *Experimental and quasi-experimental design for research.* Chicago: Rand McNally.

> *Classic book on the designs used to structure surveys and the research studies that include them. Because design and sampling interact, this book is a valuable resource.*

Creative Research Systems. (2001). *The survey system.* Online at www.sur-
    veysystem.com.

Offers a step-by-step guide to calculating sample size.

Dillman, D. A. (1978). *Mail and telephone surveys: The total design method.* New
    York: John Wiley.

Reviews the special issues associated with mail and telephone surveys.

Frey, J. H. (1989). *Survey research by telephone* (2nd ed.). Newbury Park, CA:
    Sage.

*Contains a good review of the sampling questions that telephone surveys
raise.*

Henry, G. T. (1990). *Practical sampling.* Newbury Park, CA: Sage.

*Excellent source of information about sampling methods and sampling
errors. Readers with knowledge of statistics will find this book most helpful,
but it is worthwhile even for readers whose statistical knowledge is basic.*

Kish, L. (1965). *Survey sampling.* New York: John Wiley.

*A classic book, useful for resolving issues that arise when sampling designs
are implemented.*

Kraemer, H. C., & Thiemann, S. (1987). *How many subjects? Statistical power
    analysis in research.* Newbury Park, CA: Sage.

*Thoroughly discusses the complexity of statistical power analysis; requires
an understanding of statistics.*

Lavrakas, P. (1993). *Telephone survey methods: Sampling, selection, and supervision*
    (2nd ed.). Newbury Park, CA: Sage.

Important book for anyone interested in conducting telephone surveys.

Rossi, P. H., Wright, S. D., Fisher, G. A., & Willis, G. (1987). The urban home-
    less: Estimating composition and size. *Science, 235,* 1336-1341.

*Scholarly article discusses the difficulties of doing research with the urban
homeless.*

Trochim, W. M. K. (2000). *The research methods knowledge base* (2nd ed.).
    Cincinnati, OH: Atomic Dog.

*Comprehensive textbook (available online at trochim.human.cornell.edu/kb)
that addresses all of the topics in a typical introductory undergraduate or*

graduate course in social research methods. Covers the entire research process, including formulating research questions and research design.

University of California, Los Angeles, Department of Statistics. (2002). *Statistics calculators.* Online at ebook.stat.ucla.edu.

Internet site with links to many step-by-step guides to calculating sample size.

Glossary

Alpha value—The probability of rejecting the null hypothesis when it is actually true. Tradition keeps the alpha value small—.05, .01, or .001—to avoid the rejection of a null hypothesis when it is true (and no difference exists between group means).

Cluster sampling—Sampling of naturally occurring units (such as schools or universities, which have many classrooms, students, and teachers; hospitals; cities; or states). The clusters are randomly selected, and all members of the selected cluster are included in the sample.

Convenience sample—A sample made up of individuals the researcher finds to be easily available and willing to participate.

Dependent variables—The attitudes, behaviors, and knowledge a survey is measuring. In statistical terms, these are the variables for which estimates are to be made or inferences drawn.

Effect size—The difference between the means ($\mu_1 - \mu_2$). (The effect size is based on means if the outcome is numerical, on proportions if the outcome is nominal, and on correlations if the outcome is an association. Effect sizes can also be expressed as differences between odds ratios or relative risks.)

Eligibility criteria—Characteristics (such as age, knowledge, experience) that render an individual appropriate for inclusion in the survey.

Exclusion criteria—Characteristics (e.g., too old, live too far away) that rule out certain people from participating in the survey. The survey's findings will not apply to them.

Focus group—A carefully selected group of (usually) 6 to 10 people who represent a particular population (such as teens, potential customers, or members of a particular profession) and are brought together to give their opinions and offer their perspectives on specific topics. Focus groups are often used in marketing research.

Inclusion criteria—The characteristics a person is required to have to be eligible for participation in the survey.

Independent variables—The "grouping variables" that are used to predict or explain the dependent variables.

Level of significance—The probability of rejecting the null hypothesis when it is actually true. When chosen before the test is performed, the level of significance is called the *alpha value* (see **Alpha value**).

Multistage sampling—An extension of cluster sampling in which clusters are selected and then a sample is drawn from the cluster members by simple random sampling.

Nonprobability sampling—Sampling in which some members of the eligible target population have a chance of being chosen for participation in the survey and others do not.

Null hypothesis (H_0)—A statement that no difference exists between the averages or mean scores of two groups.

***p* value**—The probability that an observed result (or result of a statistical test) is due to chance rather than to participation in a program (or exposure to some other innovation or intervention). The probability is calculated *after* the statistical test.

Probability sampling—Sampling in which every member of the target population has a known, nonzero probability of being included in the sample. Probability sampling implies the use of random selection.

Quota sampling—Sampling in which the population being studied is divided into subgroups (such as male and female, younger and older) and the numbers of subgroup members in the sample are proportional to the numbers in the larger population.

Random sampling—Sampling in which members of the target population are selected one at a time and independently. Once they have been selected, they are not eligible for a second chance and are not returned to the pool. Because of this equality of opportunity, random samples are considered relatively unbiased.

Representative sample—A sample in which important characteristics (e.g., age, gender, health status) are distributed similarly to the way they are distributed in the population at large. A representative sample is a model of the population from which it is drawn.

Response rate—The number of persons who respond (numerator) divided by the number of eligible respondents (denominator).

Sample—A portion or subset of a larger group called a *population,* which is the universe to be sampled. A good sample is a miniature version of the population.

Sampling distribution—The distribution of values formed by the means that are computed from a sample. For example, say the mean score in a survey of attitudes toward a bond issue is 50. An examination of an infinite number of means taken from an infinite number of samples would find the means clustering around 50. When the sample size reaches 30 or more, the distribution of the sampling means has the shape of the normal distribution.

GLOSSARY

Sampling error (or bias)—Variation of the sample means around the true value. The sample means tend to gather closer around the true population mean with larger sample sizes and less variation in what is being measured.

Sampling frame—A list of the units that constitute the population from which a sample is to be selected. If the sample is to be representative, all members of the population must be included on the sampling frame.

Sampling unit—An individual, group, or other entity that is selected for the survey or assigned to a group.

Snowball sampling—Sampling that relies on previously identified members of a group to identify other members of the population.

Standard deviation—A common measure of the dispersion or spread of the data around the mean.

Standard error of the mean—A statistic used to describe the sampling error. The difference between the standard deviation and the standard error of the mean is that the standard deviation tells how much variability can be expected among individuals. The standard error of the mean is the standard deviation of the means in a sampling distribution. It tells how much variability can be expected among means in future samples.

Stratified random sampling—A sampling method in which the population is divided into subgroups, or "strata," and a sample is then randomly selected from each subgroup.

Systematic sampling—A sampling method in which every nth (5th or 10th or 12th, and so on) name is selected from a list of eligible survey subjects.

Target population—All individuals to whom the survey is to apply; a sample is drawn from the target population.

Type I error—The form of error that occurs when differences are found to exist between two groups although in reality there are no differences; also called *alpha error.*

Type II error—The form of error that occurs when no differences are found between groups although in reality there are differences; also called *beta error.*

Unit of analysis—The entity whose survey data are examined statistically.

GLOSSARY

About the Author

Arlene Fink, Ph.D., is Professor of Medicine and Public Health at the University of California, Los Angeles. She is on the Policy Advisory Board of UCLA's Robert Wood Johnson Clinical Scholars Program, a consultant to the UCLA-Neuropsychiatric Institute Health Services Research Center, and President of Arlene Fink Associates, a research and evaluation company. She has conducted surveys and evaluations throughout the United States and abroad and has trained thousands of health professionals, social scientists, and educators in survey research, program evaluation, and outcomes and effectiveness research. Her published works include more than 100 articles, books, and monographs. She is co-author of *How to Conduct Surveys: A Step-by-Step Guide* and author of *Evaluation Fundamentals: Guiding Health Programs, Research, and Policy; Evaluation for Education and Psychology;* and *Conducting Literature Reviews: From Paper to the Internet.*